Leo Tolstoy and Jesus Christ

By Gene Allen Groner

To the memory of the 56 million people in the world who die every year, and for the blessing of their families and friends left behind.

May they all rest in peace, through Jesus Christ our Savior and friend, amen.

To

From

Other Books and eBooks by Gene Allen Groner

Journey of a Disciple

The Garden of Eden

Native American Prayers Poems and Legends

Native American Horses

Native American Fine Art

Micah's Fine Art

Fine Art by Sassan Filsoof

Son of the Most High

These Three Remain

The Helper: a Discourse on the Holy Spirit

Hallowed Be Thy Name

Deborah: Prophetess and Warrior

Saint Teresa of Calcutta

From Shepherd to King: the Story of David

The Nature of Angels

Speak To This People: Bible Prophets

For Such a Time as This: the Story of Esther

Prayers and Poems of Christ

In the Beginning

Take Off Your Sandals, the story of Moses

The Silver-Tongued Prophet: Isaiah

My God is Yahweh: the Story of Elijah

Meditations

Evangelist Billy Graham

World's Greatest Missionary

Stairway to Heaven

2020 Poems

Full of Grace

Jesus' Hands Are Kind Hands

The Kingdom of Heaven

Genesis to Revelation: Women in the Bible

Testify

Revelation

The Cross

The Road to Emmaus

Pentecost

The Mount of Beatitudes

The Resurrection of Lazarus

Leo Tolstoy and Christ

Introduction

This is a miracle that could only come from God.

Last night I lay awake for an hour or so, thinking about what book I should write next, after I had just finished writing The Resurrection of Lazarus.

No results, nothing came to mind. So I drifted off to sleep and awoke at 5 am with the idea clearly on my mind to write about Leo Tolstoy—a totally ridiculous idea, because I am a Christian writer who writes books and articles about the Bible and people who are in the Bible.

The first book I wrote was my autobiography titled, Journey of a Disciple. Other biographies I've written are about Jesus, Moses, Elijah, John the Baptist, and Mary the Mother of Jesus.

I write about prayer, faith, spirituality, nature, poetry, and fine art.

Why would the thought of writing about Leo Tolstoy come into my mind this morning? It makes no sense—the Russian author of War and Peace, really? It must be something I ate.

So after I ate breakfast, I went straight to my laptop and looked up Leo Tolstoy, and to my complete astonishment, I began reading about his "spiritual awakening" and relationship with Jesus Christ.

But that's not all. The title of his book, Resurrection, literally took my breath away!

Resurrection is the topic of the book I just finished writing—The Resurrection of Lazarus.

There is no such thing as coincidence where God is concerned. It's a God-thing. Plain and simple, a God-thing. Without a doubt, a God-thing.

"God works in mysterious ways, his wonders to perform."

So here's my latest book. I hope you like it. I think that would please our Creator. Amen.

Chapter One

Count Lev Nikolayevich Tolstoy

His Russian name is Lev Nikolayevich Tolstoy. In English he is called Leo Tolstoy.

Count Lev Tolstoy was born in 1828 into a wealthy Russian family of noblemen. He is known as one of the greatest writers of all time, and was nominated for the Nobel Prize in Literature four times, the Nobel Peace Prize three times.

He is most famous for his novels War and Peace, which I read many years ago, and for Anna Karenina, which has been made into a movie I plan to watch this year.

Tolstoy has authored numerous novels, novellas, short stories, and philosophical essays—a prolific writer to say the least.

As I mentioned in the introduction to this book, he authored his non-fiction work, A Confession in 1882, following his "spiritual awakening."

He wrote about Jesus and focused on Christ's teachings from the Sermon on the Mount, which I wrote about in my recent book The Mount of Beatitudes.

In 1894 Tolstoy wrote The Kingdom of God Is Within You, in which he proclaimed his pacifist position of non-violent resistance. This idea and philosophy had a profound influence on Mahatma Gandhi and Dr. Martin Luther King, Jr. in their efforts to build peace among their people and the world.

He wrote his last and longest full-length novel in 1899, titled Resurrection, which I mentioned in my introduction. In the book Resurrection, Tolstoy wrote about the differences between the teachings of Jesus and the way people were in the church, and about the apparent injustices of the laws of man versus the laws of God our Creator.

The book Resurrection was translated into English as The Awakening (as in Tolstoy's spiritual awakening). The novel is about a man named Dmitri Ivanovich Nekhlyudov, a Russian nobleman who is hoping to find forgiveness and redemption for his previous sins. Though I haven't yet read Resurrection, I have it on my to-do list of books to read.

Although Resurrection outsold both Anna Karenina and War and Peace, it is not as well-known as those two novels. Published as a full-length fiction novel in 1936, some have said it serves as the archetype for all melodrama.

Made into a film by directors in China, Italy, and America, the most popular version is the film by Samuel Goldwyn's We Live Again, filmed in 1934 with Fredric March and Anna Sten. I would like to see it if I can hopefully find it somewhere.

Chapter Two

Leo Tolstoy and the Sermon on the Mount

Leo Tolstoy believed that Jesus' Sermon on the Mount is the best thing the Bible has to offer. He saw it as the basis for Christianity and Jesus' moral teachings to his disciples and the church.

Tolstoy criticized both the state and the institutional church for not living up to the moral code that he felt was only right—right not only for the church, but for the state as well.

He saw the violence with which the state treated its citizens, and he knew that violence only created more violence. He also knew that the teachings of Jesus from his Sermon on the Mount were opposed to violence. Tolstoy pointed to the passage in Matthew which he strongly believed in, Matthew 5:38-42.

In the King James Version it reads as follows:

Jesus said, "Ye have heard that it hath been said, An eye for an eye, and a tooth for a tooth:
But I say unto you, That ye resist not evil: but whosoever shall smite thee on thy right cheek, turn to him the other also.

"And if any man will sue thee at the law, and take away thy coat, let him have thy cloak also.

And whosoever shall compel thee to go a mile, go with him twain.

Give to him that asketh thee, and from him that would borrow of thee turn not thou away."

This was Leo Tolstoy's summation of the principles of Christianity to which he subscribed. He felt the state and the church should live by the principles of Jesus' teachings from the Sermon on the Mount.

This was Tolstoy's religion. In his mind this was revolutionary. It was how Jesus taught that everyone should respond to evil in this manner, and it formed the basis for Tolstoy's pacifism and non-violence which he believed and which he wrote about in his book Resurrection, and in his subsequent book What I Believe.

Chapter Three

What I Believe

For Tolstoy, love is the answer. It is the correct response to violence and the right way to live in all our relationships.

In his book titled What I Believe, pages 18 and 19, he has this to say:

"It may be affirmed that the constant fulfilment of this rule is difficult, and that not every man will find his happiness in obeying it. It may be said that it is foolish; that, as unbelievers pretend, Jesus was a visionary, an idealist, whose impracticable rules were only followed because of the stupidity of his disciples. But it is impossible not to admit that Jesus did say very clearly and definitely that which he intended to say: namely, that men should not resist evil; and that therefore he who accepts his teaching cannot resist. Hence, according to Tolstoy, only hypocrites deny that the crux of Jesus' teaching was to call for non-resistance to (whatever gets defined as) evil.

He believed that Christians should follow Jesus' teaching, and that if they did that there would be no need for the state. Everyone would have all their needs met, and people would take care of each other. The state would not be needed.

He believed that the state and the institutionalized church used lies and deceit to control the populace, to exercise their power over them. The church, he said, uses rituals and superstition to control the people, in the same way that the state uses violence for power and control.

Radical and revolutionary views as they were, it must be remembered that Tolstoy lived in a time when that is what he predominantly witnessed. It was the way things were then in Russia in the late 1800s.

For Tolstoy, the church and the state were neither one displaying the Christian virtues that Jesus expounded in the Sermon on the Mount. They were both bound, he believed, to become obsolete and defunct since they failed to demonstrate the kind of Christianity that he understood Jesus of Nazareth would approve.

The many books he wrote during the latter part of his life were devoted to exposing the religious and political corruption which he saw and heard from them. And although he was censored repeatedly for his writing, his books and essays continued to circulate both within the state of Russia and in other countries.

Chapter Four

Rational Christianity

Today, many people would denounce the religious views of Leo Tolstoy. He certainly was correct in criticizing the state and church of his day for their denial of the teachings of Jesus' Sermon on the Mount, however, Tolstoy's ideas are primarily based on a rationalistic approach to the teaching of Jesus Christ.

He considered Jesus to be a very rational person. He failed to see Jesus as the Son of God, born of a virgin, resurrected from the grave, and bound for heaven to dwell with God. Jesus, he believed, had the best ideas on morality that had ever been brought forth.

The code of Jesus, especially that which was presented in the Sermon on the Mount, was eloquent and the best model of Christianity in existence. Everything miraculous and mysterious Tolstoy relegated to the realm of superstition and wishful thinking. He did not believe in life after death, or in eternal life.

Rather, he did believe that the Christianity of Jesus Christ offered the best hope for humanity. This gave Tolstoy hope for the future and a purpose for living—meani

Though Tolstoy's particular sense of rational Christianity would make today's Christians very uncomfortable, nevertheless his views still hold a significant place in Christian literature. That is especially true of Christian literature that is anarchist and solely that of Jesus Christ.

He felt the Bible mostly camouflaged the rational Christianity of Jesus, Jesus true and basic message of morality. Everything else is merely a smokescreen to the reality Tolstoy believed and wrote about.

Chapter Five

Tolstoy's Life and His Career as an Author

Leo Tolstoy was the fourth son of the five children born to Count Nikolai Ilyich Tolstoy (1794–1837) and Countess Mariya Tolstaya (née Volkonskaya; 1790–1830).

His parents died when he was just a child. His mother died when he was only two, and his father died when Leo was only the age of nine.

The teachers at Kazan University said he was uncooperative and not able to learn.

At the University, Tolstoy studied Oriental Languages and the Law. When he left the University, he lived in Moscow and Saint Petersburg. There he began his writing career.

In the military service, he was an Artillery Officer who was given high honors in courage and bravery. However, he never cared for all the deaths and the killing. After the Crimean War Tolstoy left the military to resume his writing career.

During the war he traveled throughout Europe, and all of the killing he witnessed and participated in helped him define his future life as a non-violent pacifist, which he wrote about extensively throughout the remainder of his life.

Tolstoy met Victor Hugo in 1861 and read Hugo's Les Miserables with great enthusiasm. His reading of Les Miserables no doubt

contributed to his authorship of his most famous War and Peace.

Leo Tolstoy married Sophia Andreyevna Behrs in September of 1862. Born in 1844, she was sixteen years younger than Tolstoy. Sonya, as she was called by family and friends, was one of three daughters of German physician Andrey Evstafievich Behrs and his Russian wife Liubov Alexandrovna. They were married in Moscow.

Together they had 13 children, five of them dying in childhood.

Leo Tolstoy as a Young Man

Tolstoy's Wife Sophia, with Daughter Alexandra

Though Leo Tolstoy and Sophia started life as a happy couple with happy children, his radical interpretation of Christianity and the state took its toll on their marriage and family life during the later years. Some have even said that their marriage and family life deteriorated to the point of extreme unhappiness for both of them.

It was during this period in their lives that Tolstoy renounced his family fortune and the copyrights to his novels.

Following the Russian Revolution in 1905, many members of Tolstoy's family rejected the newly formed Soviet Union. They and their descendants moved to other countries— Sweden, the United Kingdom, and the United States.

His cousin Anna remained and later became a famous Russian journalist and television host.

Chapter Six

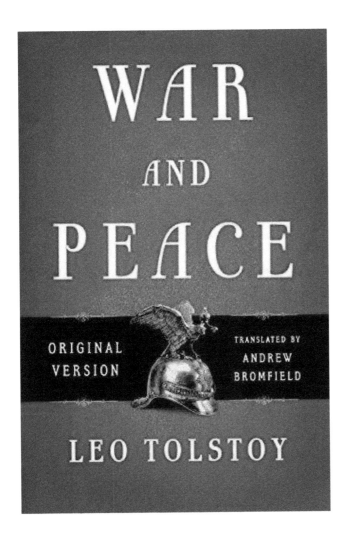

The Novels of Leo Tolstoy

Tolstoy's Novels and Novellas

Leo Tolstoy in 1897 at the Age of 69

Tolstoy's best-known novels are War and Peace and Anna Karenina, and the shorter novels, known as novellas, which include The Cossacks, Hadji Murad and The Death of Ivan Ilyich.

War and Peace was published as a complete novel in 1869. It has always been acknowledged as one of his greatest works, a true masterpiece and a classic.

The story in this historical novel takes place during the French invasion of Russia, known as the Patriotic War of 1812. Napoleon's army had crossed the Neman River in Russia on June 24 in an attempt to overtake the Russian Army..

The novel is written from the point of view of several aristocratic and well-to-do families. The main characters of which are introduced at a party in St. Petersburg in 1805. The families of the Bezukhovs, Bolkonskys, and the Rostovs provide the main interactions in the novel.

The Russian emperor Alexander I signs a peace treaty with France in 1807. However, when Napoleon invades Russia, Tsar Alexander is forced to declare war.

The French defeat is a turning point in the Napoleonic Wars. At the same time, it helps solidify the Russian dominance in eastern Europe and the world, a fact of history we are still dealing with today.

Tolstoy never considered War and Peace a novel. He felt that Anna Karenina was truly his first novel. In 1863 he began writing War and Peace, and it reached publication in several

parts over the subsequent six years of Tolstoy's writing it, first beginning as a series of magazine articles published in the Russian periodical Russkiy Vestnik under the title 1805. The series wasn't widely received at the time, and Tolstoy and Sophia decided to discontinue the series and seek publication of the entire work as a novel.

The prominent artist Mikhail Bashilov was hired to illustrate the novel. Three volumes were published by 1868. Sales of the novel were promising, and three more volumes were subsequently completed by 1869, and eventually the entire work was completed with 1200 pages—a lengthy novel to be sure.

War and Peace has been translated into at least 10 different languages. The first half of the novel is mainly fictional with fictional characters, while the second half of the novel deals with the study of history, war, and power.

As a historical novel dealing with the Napoleonic Wars and a philosophy of history, the novel is unparalleled. The biographies of fictional characters makes the lengthy work interesting and colorful, with love, romance, mystery, and adventure holding the reader's attention until the very end—an altogether fascinating read.

As I think about Leo Tolstoy, I am reminded of the circumstance in which I became a writer.

Let me tell you my personal testimony of how and why I began writing.

Not long ago, I was in a Christian bookstore in Independence, Missouri. Looking through the displays, I noticed a new book written by Mark Batterson titled, Draw the Circle. The title was catchy, so I picked it up and looked through the pages, until I fell upon a particular page where the author issued a challenge. I'm always up to new challenges, so I read on.

The challenge read as follows: Pray on your knees at the same time every day for 40 days and watch for the miracles that come to you. Wow! I thought. I have prayed all my life, but not on my knees, so I thought I might give it a try and see what happens. I was in one of those down cycles that Christians get in to from time to time, and I needed a boost—a spark in my heart that could ignite a flame of passion for life once again.

That night, as I was preparing for bed, I remembered the book and the challenge. So I took off my shoes—Moses was told to do this in the Exodus out of respect for God—and knelt beside my bed to pray. I said, "Dear Lord, I am

accepting this challenge and I ask for your perfect will to be done in my life. May I once again feel the flame of passion for life. I am willing to do whatever you want me to do. In Jesus' name, amen."

For the next 40 days I prayed this same prayer in the same way. On the morning of the 41st day, I awoke early with the thought in my mind to write a book. I had never written a book before, so this would be a new experience for me. Believing it might be the Lord who planted that idea in my mind, I went to my computer and opened up Microsoft Word to begin. As I did so, the words started to flow from my mind on to the pages, and I haven't stopped writing since that day. Day after day, word after word, I write one Christian book, blog, or magazine article after another. The Lord has given me a fresh new lease on life and a passion for writing that I love.

It is now 2020 and I have written and published more than 40 Christian books, in addition to a number of magazine articles on faith and spirituality. I am amazed at how the Holy Spirit continues to bring me ideas and empowers me to write, sharing my testimony of the peace and love of Our Lord and Savior Jesus Christ. Thanks be to God.

It all began with a simple prayer. The reason I write is to witness of the love and grace of

Jesus Christ, and the building up of God's kingdom here on earth. All the honor and glory goes to God, the Father of us all, and I am more than happy to give him all the credit—he deserves it all. I am reminded of the Christian song by William and Gloria Gaither titled, "Jesus is Lord of All."

"Lord of all, Lord of all, Jesus is Lord of all. All my possessions and all my life, Jesus is Lord of all."

The greatest desire of my heart is for the testimony of Jesus' love and peace to go to every person and every nation on earth, doing my part to help fulfill the Great Commission,

 "Therefore go and make disciples of all nations, baptizing them in the name of the Father and of the Son and of the Holy Spirit, and teaching them to obey everything I have commanded you. And surely I am with you always, to the very end of the age." (Matthew 28:19-20 NIV)

Chapter Seven

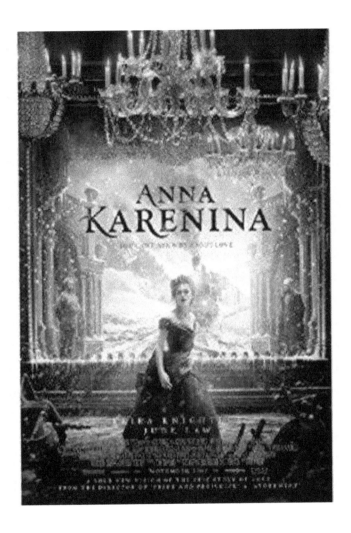

Anna Karenina the Novel

First published in 1978, Tolstoy considered Anna Karenina his first novel.

The novel covers a vast panorama of Russian life in the 19th century, as well as human nature itself. With vivid imagination and skillful use of words and phrases, Tolstoy has indeed created a masterpiece, perhaps his best one.

The novel contains over 800 pages, and is filled with major characters—more than a dozen of them filling the book in eight parts.

The colorful characters begin with Anna, frustrated and unhappy wife of Karenin, who falls in passionate love with cavalry officer Count Alexei Kirillovich Vronsky. A sophisticated woman, Anna finds the outlet for her passions in the handsome Count.

The news of their affair rocks St. Petersburg, and the couple is forced to relocate to Italy.

Upon their later return to Russia, the couple finds their lives in a turmoil.

The 1967 screen version, which opened in the Soviet Union, featured Tatiana Samoilova, pictured above.

Portrait of Anna Karenina from the National Museum in Warsaw

Tolstoy was unhappy with his first drafts of Anna Karenina, and wrote in his journal, "I loathe what I have written. The galleys of Anna Karenina for the April issue of Russkij Vestnik now lie on my table, and I really don't have the heart to correct them. Everything in them is so rotten, and the whole thing should be rewritten—all that has been printed too—scrapped, and melted down, thrown away, renounced.

As a writer, I can understand some of Tolstoy's feelings of dissatisfaction. Whereas I have not had that depth of feeling about what I have written, I do go back and rewrite the books I write several times, making improvements and correcting mistakes in the manuscript. Fortunately, my books are only printed as orders come in, so I have the freedom to make revisions without increasing the cost of production. In addition, I have not felt yet that the entire work is "rotten" as expressed in his journal.

The Lord has blessed me abundantly in my writing career, and for that I am eternally grateful. God is gracious and faithful to all.

He has been with me throughout my whole life. I have a testimony to that effect I would like to share with you. It's titled, Footprints in the Sand.

Footprints in the Sand

It wasn't easy growing up without a father in my life, but it was even harder for my mother, who was faced with raising three sons by herself. I learned early on to work and help out, throwing papers, shining shoes, and selling door to door. In the summers I worked in the hayfields and cornfields. I became self-reliant at an early age. Since we couldn't depend on a dad to provide for us, I quickly learned to depend mainly on myself. As soon as I graduated from high school, I joined the Marine Corps. It was there that I learned about teamwork and the need to depend on others—they counted on me, and I counted on them. To survive and fulfill our mission, we needed each other.

After my tour in the Marines, I married and we soon had five wonderful children. My wife and children learned they could depend on me to take care of them and to provide a good living. It was during those early years that I first read the beautiful poem by Mary Fishback Powers, titled Footprints in the Sand. Looking back over my life I realize that I have never been alone. God has always been with me, carrying me through the difficult times when my own strength and self-reliance wasn't enough.

And more than that, I needed my family and all the other people in my life who have helped me when I needed strength and support. I owe God and everyone a debt of gratitude, and I give thanks to them all, especially in my later years when self-reliance just isn't enough.

The simple truth is this: we all need each other—God made us that way. We need others for love and fellowship, spiritual, emotional, and material support. It is God's way, and we wouldn't want it to be any different.

In my life there have been many "footprints in the sand." Thank you, God, for a lifetime of blessings, and for my family and friends who have walked beside me on this journey of faith. I look forward to seeing them in heaven.

Footprints

One night a man dreamed he was walking along the beach with the Lord. As scenes of his life flashed before him, he noticed that there were two sets of footprints in the sand. He also noticed at his saddest, lowest times there was one set of footprints. This bothered the man and he asked the Lord, "Did you not promise that if I gave my heart to you that you'd be with me all the way? Then, why is there only one set of footprints during my most troublesome times?" The Lord replied, "My precious child, I love you and would never forsake you. During those times of trial and suffering when you see only one set of footprints, it was then I carried you."

Jesus: "I am with you always."
MATTHEW 28:20

The novel Anna Karenina is significant to subject of this book, not only because it is by Leo Tolstoy, but also because the novel explores the themes of faith, family, fidelity, peace and commitment.

I take these themes very seriously, and try and incorporate them into my daily devotions and way of living.

Jesus took them seriously as well. His teachings from the Sermon on the Mount deal with these very things. "Blessed are the peacemakers" and "Blessed are those who hunger and thirst after righteousness" are both at the heart of Tolstoy's novel.

Do the right thing.

Live a life of peace.

"Seek first the kingdom of God and His righteousness, and all these things shall be added to you." (Matthew 6:33)

Leo Tolstoy valued and promoted the principles of Jesus, particularly his teachings from the Sermon on the Mount.

Tolstoy's values are apparent in his writing. Whether by showing the contrast between good and evil, or by stating them directly— they are there if we only look for them.

Chapter Eight

Bibliography of Leo Tolstoy

Leo Tolstoy was not a religious man. But he did believe strongly in the teaching of Jesus' Sermon on the Mount. Much of his writing is infused with these ideas, if we only look for them. One might even say that with his writing he was spreading the word of Christ.

Some of his books deal directly with subject of the teaching of Jesus Christ and the church. However, I do not mean to imply that Tolstoy saw his purpose as that of a missionary or evangelist. I am speaking in the broadest of terms.

Here is what I do know about him. He believed in peace and love of humanity, and believed that Jesus taught the only way for humanity to live, namely in harmony with each other and the gospel of love and peace.

If you were able to ask Leo Tolstoy "what is the secret of life and happiness?" he'd say "Love and Peace."

Leo Tolstoy and Jesus Christ have this in common—They proclaim Love and Peace.

Tolstoy was a prolific writer. Looking at his bibliography, we can quickly see the depth and breadth of his writing—writing about subjects that range from faith and family to war and peace to religion and history and politics.

Fiction and non-fiction. Novels and short stories. Dramas and plays and everything in between—a really astounding bibliography.

Here is the list as I know it today:

Novels

War and Peace (Война и мир [Voyna i mir], 1869)

Anna Karenina (Анна Каренина [Anna Karenina], 1877)

Resurrection (Воскресение [Voskresenie], 1899)

Novellas

The Autobiographical Trilogy

Childhood (Детство [Detstvo], 1852)

Boyhood (Отрочество [Otrochestvo], 1854)

Youth (Юность [Yunost'], 1856)

Family Happiness (Семейное счастье [Semeynoe schast'e], 1859)

The Cossacks (Казаки [Kazaki], 1863)

The Death of Ivan Ilyich (Смерть Ивана Ильича [Smert' Ivana Il'icha], 1886)

The Kreutzer Sonata (Крейцерова соната [Kreitserova Sonata], 1889)

The Devil (Дьявол [Dyavol] 1911, written 1889)

The Forged Coupon (Фальшивый купон [Fal'shivyi kupon], 1911)

Hadji Murat (Хаджи-Мурат [Khadzhi-Murat], 1912, 1917)

Short stories

"The Raid" ("Набег" ["Nabeg"], 1852)

"The Wood-Felling" ("Рубка леса" ["Rubka lesa"], 1855)

"Sevastopol Sketches" ("Севастопольские рассказы" ["Sevastopolskie rasskazy"], 1855–1856)

"Sevastopol in December 1854" (1855)

"Sevastopol in May 1855" (1855)

"Sevastopol in August 1855" (1856)

"A Billiard-Marker's Notes" ("Записки маркера" ["Zapiski markera"], 1855)

"The Snowstorm" ("Метель" ["Metel"], 1856)

"Two Hussars" ("Два гусара" ["Dva gusara"], 1856)

"A Landlord's Morning" ("Утро помещика", 1856)

"Lucerne" ("Люцерн" ["Lyutsern"], 1857)

"Albert" ("Альберт" ["Al'bert"], 1858)

"Three Deaths" ("Три смерти" ["Tri smerti"], 1859)

"The Porcelain Doll" (1863, a letter written with his wife to his wife's younger sister that is treated by critics as a short story)

"Polikúshka" ("Поликушка" ["Polikushka"], 1863)

"God Sees the Truth, But Waits" ("Бог правду видит, да не скоро скажет" ["Bog pravdu vidit, da ne skoro skazhet"], 1872)

"The Prisoner in the Caucasus" ("Кавказский пленник" ["Kavkazskii plennik"], 1872)

"The Bear-Hunt" (1872)

"Memoirs of a Madman" (1884)

"Croesus and Fate" (1886)

"An Old Acquaintance" (1887)

"Kholstomer" ("Холстомер", 1888)

"A Lost Opportunity" (1889)

"Françoise" ("Франсуаза", 1891, alteration of Guy de Maupassant's "Port")

"A Talk Among Leisured People" (1893)

"Walk in the Light While There is Light" (1893)

"The Coffee-House of Surrat" ("Суратская кофейная", 1893)

"The Young Tsar" (1894)

"Master and Man" ("Хозяин и работник" ["Khozyain and rabotnik"], 1895)

"Too Dear!" ("Дорого стоит" ["Dorogo stoit"], 1897)

"Father Sergius" ("Отец Сергий" ["Otetz Sergij"], 1898)

"The Long Exile" (1899)

"Work, Death, and Sickness" (1903)

"Three Questions" ("Три вопроса" ["Tri voprosa"], 1903)

"After the Ball" ("После бала" ["Posle bala"], (1903)

"The Posthumous Notes of the Starets Feodor Kuzmich" ("Посмертные записки старца

Федора Кузьмича") (Unfinished, 1905, published in 1912)

"Alyosha the Pot" ("Алёша Горшок" ["Alyosha Gorshok"], 1905)

"Divine and Human" ("Божеское и человеческое", 1906)

"What For?" ("За что?", 1906)

"There Are No Guilty People" (1909)

"Three Days in the Village" ("Три дня в деревне", non-fictional sketch, 1910)

"Khodynka: An Incident of the Coronation of Nicholas II" ("Ходынка", 1910)

"My Dream" ("Что я видел во сне", 1911)

Stories that have not been translated into English:

"Разжалованный" (1856)

"Две лошади" (1880)

"Прыжок" (1880)

"Рассказ Аэронавта" (1880)

"Карма" (1894)

"Бедные люди" (1905)

"Корней Васильев" (1906)

"Ягоды" (1906)

"Благодарная почва" (1910)

"Разговор с прохожим" (1910, written 1909)

"Песни на деревне" (1910, written 1909)

"Идиллия" (1911, written 1861-62)

"Кто прав?" (1911, written 1891—1893)

"Отец Василий" (1911, written 1906)

"Нечаянно" (1911, written 1910)

"Сон молодого царя" (1912, written 1894)

"Сила детства" (1912, written 1908)

"Проезжий и крестьянин" (1917, written 1909)

"История вчерашнего дня" (1928, written 1851)

"Святочная ночь" (1928, written 1853)

"Как умирают русские солдаты" (1928, written 1854)

"Отрывки рассказов из деревенской жизни" (1932, written 1860—1862)

Fables

"What Men Live By" ("Чем люди живы" ["Chem lyudi zhivy"], 1881)

"Ilyás" ("Ильяс", 1885)

"Where Love Is, God Is" ("Где любовь, там и бог", 1885)

"Evil Allures, But Good Endures" ("Вражье лепко, а божье крепко", 1885)

"Wisdom of Children" ("Девчонки умнее стариков", 1885)

"Quench the Spark" ("Упустишь огонь, не потушишь" ["Upustish ogon', ne potushish"], 1885)

"Two Old Men" ("Два старика", 1885)

"The Candle" ("Свечка", 1886)

"Ivan the Fool" ("Сказка об дураке", 1885)

"The Three Hermits" ("Три Старца", 1886)

"Promoting a Devil" ("Как чертёнок краюшку выкупал", 1886)

"Repentance" ("Кающийся грешник", 1886)

"The Grain" ("Зерно с куриное яйцо", 1886)

"How Much Land Does a Man Need?" ("Много ли человеку земли нужно", 1886)

"The Godson" ("Крестник", 1886)

"The Empty Drum" ("Работник Емельян и пустой барабан", 1891)

"The Restoration of Hell" ("Разрушение ада и восстановление его", 1903, written 1902)

"Esarhaddon, King of Assyria" ("Ассирийский царь Асархадон", 1903)

Fables that have not been translated into English:

"Два брата и золото" (1886, written 1885)

"Три сына" (1889, written 1887)

"Три притчи" (1895)

"Две различные версии истории улья с лубочной крышкой" (1912, written 1900)

"Волк" (1909, written 1908)

Plays

The Power of Darkness (Власть тьмы [Vlast' t'my], 1886)

The First Distiller (1886)

The Light Shines in Darkness (1890)

The Fruits of Enlightenment (Плоды просвещения [Plody prosvesheniya], 1891)

The Living Corpse (Живой труп [Zhivoi trup], 1900)

The Cause of it All (1910)

Non-fiction

Philosophical works

A Confession (1879) – Volume 1 of an untitled four-part work[1]

A Criticism of Dogmatic Theology (1880) – Volume 2 of an untitled four-part work

The Gospel in Brief, or A Short Exposition of the Gospel (1881)

The Four Gospel Unified and Translated (1881) – Volume 3 of an untitled four-part work

Church and State (1882)

What I Believe (also called My Religion) (1884) – Volume 4 of an untitled four-part work

What Is to Be Done? (also translated as What Then Must We Do?) (1886)

On Life (1887)

The Love of God and of One's Neighbour (1889)

Supplementary essay for Timofei Bondarev's The Triumph of the Farmer or Industry and Parasitism (1888)

Why Do Men Intoxicate Themselves? (1890)

The First Step: on vegetarianism (1892)[2]

The Kingdom of God Is Within You (1893)

Non-Activity (1893)

The Meaning of Refusal of Military Service (1893)

Reason and Religion (1894)

Religion and Morality (1894)

Christianity and Patriotism (1894)

Non-Resistance: letter to Ernest H. Crospy (1896)

How to Read the Gospels (1896)

The Deception of the Church (1896)

Letter to the Liberals[3] (1898)

Christian Teaching (1898)

On Suicide (1900)

The Slavery of Our Times (1900)

Thou Shalt Not Kill (1900)

Reply to the Holy Synod (1901)

The Only Way (1901)

On Religious Toleration (1901)

What Is Religion and What is its Essence? (1902)

To the Orthodox Clergy (1903)

Bethink Yourselves! (1904)

Thoughts of Wise Men (compilation; 1904)

The Only Need (1905)

The Grate Sin (1905)

A Cycle of Reading (compilation; 1906)

Do Not Kill (1906)

Love Each Other (1906)

An Appeal to Youth (1907)

The Law of Love and the Law of Violence (1908)[1]

The Only Command (1909)

A Calendar of Wisdom (Путь Жизни [Put' Zhizni]; compilation; 1909)

Works on art and literature

The Works of Guy de Maupassant (1894)

What Is Art? (1897)

Art and Not Art (1897)

Shakespeare and the Drama (1909)

Articles, publicism

Meaningless aspirations (Бессмысленные мечтания [Bessmyslennye mechtaniya], 1895)

I can't be silent (Не могу молчать [Ne mogu molchat'], 1908)

Pedagogical works

Articles from Tolstoy's journal on education, "Yasnaya Polyana" (1861–1862)

A Primer (1872)

On Popular Instruction (1874)

A New Primer (1875)

Biography

Gene Allen Groner is a Christian writer and the author of more than 40 books and numerous articles on faith and spirituality. He lives in Independence, Missouri with his wife of 55 years, a retired public health nurse. His interests include reading and writing, gardening, and volunteer work in the community. He is listed in Who's Who in Missouri, and is a lifetime member of the National Honor Society in Psychology, Psi Chi.

Gene earned both the Bachelor and Master's Degrees with honors from Park University in Parkville, Missouri. He also attended the University of Hawaii and Saint Paul School of Theology. He and his family are lifetime members of the Colonial Hills congregation in Blue Springs, Missouri.

https://www.amazon.com/Gene-Allen-Groner/e/B077YTVSJZ

email: geneallengroner@gmail.com